DAY *for* NIGHT

RICHARD DEMING

DAY *for* NIGHT

Published in the United Kingdom in 2016 by Shearsman Books Ltd
50 Westons Hill Drive
Emersons Green
Bristol BS16 7DF
www.shearsman.com

Shearsman Books Ltd Registered Office
30–31 St. James Place, Mangotsfield, Bristol BS16 9JB
(this address not for correspondence)

ISBN 978-1-84861-485-7

DESIGN   Megan Mangum, Words That Work
COVER   Anna Conway, *It's not going to happen like that* (detail), 2013, Oil on linen.
          Courtesy of Collezione Maramotti.

TABLE OF CONTENTS

ACKNOWLEDGEMENTS

Some of these poems appeared in the following online and print journals: *American Letters and Commentary, The Berlin Journal, Boog City, Broome Street Review, Colorado Review, The Equalizer, Eyewear, Free Verse, The Iowa Review, Mandorla, Molossus, The Nation, New Haven Review, TAB*, and *WebConjunctions*.

Grateful acknowledgement is made to the American Academy in Berlin for a fellowship, during which many of these poems were either written or revised.

I.

FILM THREAT

(after George Romero, Takashi Miike, and Sam Raimi)

I.

The survivors barricade a bay window with plywood, an old armoire, an empty refrigerator and it is dark enough within to read by candlelight. Through a crack you can see two eyes and a mouth in shadow and a night filled with intent, glittering teeth. What the image tells us—that the hunger of the zombie, however slow, does not sleep, that the cottage and everyone in it is surrounded by rage, and inside no one will admit the possibility of cowardice aloud, even as the wine is decanted, the cream sauce simmers, and Mendelssohn plays on a stereo somewhere in the background. But maybe we have it wrong. The dead do not hate the living; love hates the dead for being dead and again and again summons them back. One day, and soon, the boards will come down and the zombies will break in and devour everything in their path and yet someone will raise a shotgun and shoot the beloved who is no longer the beloved but something else, some other wanton form that wears a recognizable face and someone in the audience will wonder if that is how we are meant to survive our memories.

2.

If a black phone sits on an apartment floor, then a middle-aged widower will surprise himself placing a call and then he's been alone for seven years; then on the other side of the city, another phone will ring nine times—each a small and reasonable amount of faith; then on the other end a shy, beautiful woman with black hair will answer. If she answers, then she is dressed all in white, and kneels on the floor. Then she will tell him, with her quiet and open voice, she is surprised that he would call. Then her head hangs down as she speaks, her long hair covering her face almost completely. If there are no windows where she is, then she does not yet know he has already lied to her out of his sadness. Then he does not know she has been kneeling, alone, for hours. Then they will make plans to meet for dinner and then she will smile and she will hang up the receiver. Then he will be relieved and excited and so then, in the room just beyond the black phone, a body inside a canvas bag cinched closed suddenly struggles one last moment, then stops. If so, and knowing we know that, we do not avert our eyes, do not stop listening, then there are such terrible, such familiar thirsts. These do not hide for long, no matter how white a dress may be or how many times a phone might ring, and so it cannot end well.

3.

What is it we don't do well enough that we're constantly afraid? For the insomniac, night is a book that will not stop letting itself be read. Now it's too late. A young couple, beautiful but not too bright, arrives in a yellow Oldsmobile. And when some uninvited rage rushes toward the door, anyone else would know not to open it. There will be a botched incantation and someone won't survive because the words went wrong.

In an empty room, in the coldest shadows of some forgotten house, an older man's voice echoes on a reel-to-reel. He is a disappointed father who tells a secret history over and over and who, once, long ago, was rent asunder by voices in an empty cellar. *Remember me.* Startled anew, don't ask why it's always like this. You already foresee an answer with bared teeth. And those hungers beneath the stairs will not close their eyes. Each of us a small, nearly forgotten body spinning and falling like a long kiss or a bad dream or the sound of celluloid catching fire.

RASHOMON AFFECT

In *Rashomon* the rain
                    does not sleep, sounds
          like ink-blackened pages, turning, then
                    unwriting themselves.

In the unrecognizably literal forest
          likeness is like falling,
                    like catching,
                    like falling.
                              It is human nature to fall
                    into the middle of events.

What matters is that in the tale someone's dead,
                    murdered,
                              tied to a post and words unsaid.
Some arctic continent of unspeakable
                    resentment opens wide round.

Mifune conjures close a relentless ghost, deeper
than you think,
          and who'll speak for it?—That's where you come in.

Remember me remember
                    what is here
                    what is white what is true
                    what is heat.

As you turn to go,
the weave of threadbare scrolls goes slack—
the day becomes a draft of disdain
no one can bear.
Still, it moves:
Look/tell, look/tell, look/tell.

In what follows, everyone left until the room spun
against its own
unblinking. Not even the story
owns its own
moment.

And, later, who would not wish

in the want-nothing light
to wear a face
just like
the rain in *Rashomon*.

SPEAK AT THIS

In a clear
chromosomal light
of sudden departure,

the tongue becomes an unlikely weight.

There are hours when songs will not come,
      in grief or joy, or in the startled whirlwind
          when we don't trust any love.

Not nothing now, some silence attests
what more, what noun
does not do.

That is to say, syllables coordinate vanishing
in the ledger of lost chances.

Try this:
If an apple, then exile;
a pomegranate? Then wintering descent;

a glance backward, and the pupils of the eyes
become a banishment.

What Echo said was
      a name not
      worth repeating.

And thus a beautiful daughter
slides her thumb along her lower lip.

It blooms, it shatters.

THE LAST OF NEW ENGLAND

(after Derek Jarman)

A curtain and faint, diffused light.

Begin, here:
The phone rings and someone is listening, and some cold
voice articulates
an autumn day as homesickness tightens
ligature or bond,
and then the blood,
and then the bone.

Where is the world that built me, fashioned
the knot of affection and doubt behind my left iris?

On the desk beneath
the window is a leather book,
a paperclip, the photo
of a bearded singer leaning his head
against the wall of some boarded tenement.
He does not look at the camera while at his lip
the cigarette's ash and filter
is the open mouth of a September morning.
These lead me back to where

in unpainted rooms with wooden chairs
we learned slow hymns and

                    plaintive uncertainties
to weave a present tense out of so much loss.

Dispatches from the coast:
fatigue is a river—
        the Merrimack, Charles, Concord,
        Connecticut, Housatonic,
        each one an *inter alia* of reckoning
        that breaks for the sea
                and some last best wish.

        Inside a shabby apartment,
        place your face against
        cool kitchen tiles,
        black and white,

cracked toward the direction of the fault lines
that keep the widow awake and pacing the roof. Can she
see the milk-white sin beyond all reason?
                In any given direction, a mast,
                a merry pole, a charred smoke
        stack, remote
                and without shadow.
        There's always a way into a house.

The calendar reads X and X and X and O.
I want to say *sky*, say *table*, say *tomorrow and last week*,
to voice some lenten contentment,
the odd orison of strength and retreat.

But some days the arch of the left hand sustains
     a paltry curse against half-closed doors.
The arm of a corpse catches
on the branches along the riverbank.

The last lee shore looms close by and the words you sent
     and the frosty torchlight passes
      over the back alley where
       the ransom tree counts out scars and debts.
         There is no green like that green,

which is not to say the day and all it resolves.

In sand and mortar and dread and tar and leaves.

The junkie tattoos on her cheek an *S*,
the first letter among the last days
of the telling noise of slipping out.
        Mechanisms for counting up
        the size of minor solace. I love

the cost of small talk, its shallow
owning up to a life of sundry atonement.

        The factory closes and months later
        dozens of dried chicken legs, all torn
        at the knuckle, hang
        from twine in the slow heat.

If there is a loneliness yet to be owned,
to be earned from
             wages of the half-intended

chance of belonging,
       spin the girl in the silken dress
       until the credits roll.

CARAVAGGIO DREAMS

In any place, denial, like the heart, makes itself
        known, doesn't it,
        thus, as if to say,
a tattered map belies a murderous will, or
an old story worth believing:
                                Once, a ship set forth . . .

Now, a shuttered window
frames false promises

against the fact
it is dark and it is light and
        these are not choices, but
        the most awkward invocations.

In my hand, there are five cards, all aimed toward failure,
or so go the odds.
Around the table, those who do
        not look up at
the returned man
balance the one who does.
Count the coins.

Not every outstretched hand sketches a first desire
        but Matthew, mouthing some rough plea,

calculates the very shadowed
      place that opens athwart
a younger man's smooth chest, another tongue's
Follow me that calls its moment
like the sunlight falling around some hopeful,
                    some hapless thing.

THE PICTURE OF JSB IN A PROSPECT OF LADY BOYS

I.

A hand holding a soda trembles
as some latent wish casts its lots.
The generous arch of a penciled brow
brings the gaze up close. Where else do

desires choose their changeable places?
And the one girl with an impossibly
slim waist faces the camera and smiles,
while uneven skirts sway above the knees.

In the picture there's no nearby garden
and everyone's eyes are wide open.

II.

Did you? For how much? And how must
the imagination quicken
a reality that is and is more
necessary than the one in

hand, the one we'll squint and blur
into focus. Curiosity is a kind of daily
translucence and their hair's so long,
it invents its own virtue.

Leave these be for now. Forgive me,
standing beside you, they are so lovely.

III.

There may be a future of doctors,
hormones, a shiny scalpel meant
to slit and fold because truth's
a hard thing when it's wrong.

The animal light of being
wanted is more than comfort and
persistence—the body directs
itself, everyone, all of us, along

for the ride. There's a word for
these swelling hips. Reform its
error into certain reply.

Battered by luck and the fast intent
of the dream of otherwise,
give us a song for that which bears
all it's given. Just put your lips together.

VIRTUAL REALITY

"Must / I think of everything/ as earned?"
—Robert Creeley

It is like this.

With distance and regret
cast down over open fields,
the cold shine of the stars
quickens, alters

the last light of a campfire and
its charred stones.
Ashes drift past.

SHALL I READ FROM THE HISTORY OF THE BATTLE OF THERMOPYLAE?

Now that there is nothing left, for instance,
    the taste of fear dries the upper lip.
Wood doves rustle
coppery wings along city gates. What I want is
to not want,
not you, not the scent of mango, not the livid
faces of
    fashion models, their necks arching
perversely upward.
        Not a single moment.

    The cigarette smoke's shapes auger
    thirty mornings of fraught
        silences, cold tea, the flickering
        callousness of morning
talk shows and an empty table set for three:
    for you, for me, for the polite ghost
of intensest manners.
    A quince no one will eat rolls
        behind a stove cold
            to the touch.
When things go bad, it gets like this.

        Where's the gift of sudden
    continuity?

The field of middle ground is dry.
                    Sepia-colored
                        cornstalks strewn
            all around, pointing a given
        direction. Sing out the measure

of a narrow pass. I've been lost here

before. With thumb and forefinger, blot out
                    the sun, Pilgrim. So as not
to turn my back, trembling, shine toward
            the unspeakably insistent.

            With the lights
out, it's not so far. In the movies, it's called
day for night and I will open
            my eyes to a shadow cut
in the shape of your mouth.
            In the pattern of ten stars and three
thousand
times three thousand
                    pearly eyes of gutted mackerel,
the map home is a logic
of longitude and shame.

What if you were a Persian king, cinders
            covering your forehead, your eyelashes,
            your scarred right cheek, how would
                    you arrive across a trail of broken

leaves, mercury poisonings, the ocean's systemic
threat and verdict? Would you
          take the shore
born aloft on a dozen strong backs?

And when articles of faith fashion
                    a loosened garment
          the disheveled will not return.
In the days before now, before one stretched
                    so wide round us,
I wanted a direct address,
               in something else I wanted to say
          and yet I do not know how to ask
               for fresh water,
                    for a ripened date, for
               three pomegranate seeds.

               On the last night of the sordid republic,
a soldier's wife
          waves goodbye as
                    the right nipple thickens in
               the cold, pressing
               itself against her blue t-shirt.
A bright proximity is a wrong kind of silence.

          In the garden of unregenerate narrative,
see words but think:
          arrows darkening the sky

for the unseen
       read: *loss*;
    for every comma reckon the ways
resentment can pierce the sternum
      in half. A rose leans near
    the open window and thrushes play
    at voices.

A husband runs headlong toward the river
while over his shoulder the cottage window
brackets the wife's face in an attic room.
      Drapes stir, then she's gone as
    each promise he does not keep
    drifts down
      past the walls,
          along the paths
    to the sea, there where
      children and old women
    heap up driftwood and dried seaweed
    and here is, so please it,
      where I am loved.
There are such Spartas.

IF NANCY WERE A DE KOONING

(after Joe Brainard)

On a still day surprised
        beyond all dutiful hammerings,
the skin's the color of a new plate
    or an unasked-for intuition.
Placed this
    way or that
    way, then, narrowed eyes
        shape the evidence
of my cleverest misgivings.
    In the flat back-
ground, there are thirteen types
               of blue. You
find them all.

IN A BLUE MOOD

If for a happy man the world is a happy one,
then a blue planet begets a blue heaven.

    When the music plays, I'll return
      despite myself
to the verses, the call and response,

a faith, we could say, when decisions aren't enough,
    which is so much of the time. Yet, here
        we are
    all the same, listening,
as the bass line thrums and storms.

There'll be time for evasions and glances,
for arms thrust in odd angles when the record's done.
In these measures, everything's to be found.

Let the sigh across an embouchure
call every misplaced breath back, or add a slow round
    of some piano chords and a voice that sounds
like a sky gone missing for a moment.

I'll think of you someplace framed by a window,
    backed with birdsong,
then, later, the moon, some clouds, stars. It's all I can do.

II.

AIR GUITAR

Out of the barbarous Sunday-morning
        sky a sparrow, frightened by thunder, flies again
and again into the windowpane.
        Scant questions of arrival
                and departure form under storm clouds.

My friend calls because he forgets the title of a pop tune,
mumbles some lyrics. The song begins.

        The fingers of the left hand span
        a full octave and the melody stutters and falters
against itself. The light bends away from my body.
What once was is now

some if/then conditional leading at last upstate,
        but Poughkeepsie has no harbor to anchor.
        It's all drift
                and debit.

                Around a small woodland cabin,
                rough soil is scorched
        by lightning and a boy tucks a red stone
                inside his cheek. A weight real enough
                for now.
What lasts long enough? No song, and everything
        seems elsewhere and otherwise.
        Let the unhurried apparent be

a gift to settle accounts.
I want that to be me, to place the ground,
to become the thought appearing
as a wish, a way to come back.

In a movie, the phone's plastic receiver falls to the floor.
We do not for a moment think it's a prop, a fake,
as if there were no single reason left
to lean forward, only a ghostly
address saying, "come here,
Watson, I need you" to any empty room.

The piece of leftover lamb chills in the icebox.
The rain, it raineth every goddamn day.

THE WEATHER, ALMOST

In a room upstairs, a light flickers,
then catches. A woman rehearses
the smallest glances, her voice breaking almost
to song. Eyes size up the weight
of boxes, books and pages,
                    of chipped plates of cold chicken,
        and of the beloved's head turned toward
a distant thought.

                    The throat thickens naming off losses,
            absence, the door of a house
                near the ocean remains
locked and double-bolted.

What bears its proximity?
A fireplace is filled with October ashes.

Grapes of the late season tear or burst
        yet the sugared ache of autumn fruit
        carries the mouth, you can now believe,
    through the dawn and its early frost.
        Waiting, say it so, becomes a penitent wakefulness.
What else can account our attention?

The face, that endless city—
one knows no other.

TOURNEURESQUE

(after Jacques Tourneur)

Watching a movie about a demon, I lose my way.
Demands shaped like crescent
scars narrow the focus
in a house north
     of London filled with too many midnights.

Marks on a page add up to an almost
alphabetic insistence in the book of unwanted change,

the last promise stretched
     above a dotted line.
These days are for counting down.
Some violence, call it the past, hastens
down the forest path, and it has always done so.

Beliefs strewn along the way like dolls
     with cracked porcelain heads.
I could not draw my eyes from theirs.

     And if the man with a painted face pulls
     a cyclone from his sleeve, then this bad
     begins and
what follows worse. I want a better magic.

Now, do that thing with your voice. Call it back.

WHETHER OR NOT

Then this: the house burns with a kind of panic—
        flames claim its heavy drapes,
     the banisters, soot-blackened porcelain cups
   strewn across the landing. Actions
     coin an incontestable end.

This, then, an antic landscape and above this
then, the sun is blindsided by a day-glo
     Frisbee.
                Come back, now
             come back to me. On a gray day
     voice is a lethargy. Though
         I meant to say *litany*, didn't I?
              A meaningful slip or what
       some then might call
       anger. I blink

and the morning weatherman with perfect teeth
says all conditions are
     thereby subject to change
     and you, Judas Iscariot,
     brother to shatterings uncountable,
     the grasses in the field are covered with ice:
     your dawn is unlike any other's.

This then is an eye,
     a center, the lake: what's subject
        to sudden loss.

And where is my own pale Virgil who once turned
away from the tangled woods toward
  the wide river, every drop
a forgiving, forgetful gesture?

    My name is a hollow boat. Speak it,
     then vanish.

AFTER RILKE

Once, the summer seemed an unending,
      an unspoken utterance
but now it lays shadows across sundials
and the wind steps from the field grass.

Your throat, because of the slow pollen, begins to close
and the voice is no longer recognizably
      your own.
           In the arbor,

last fruits swell and bend their branches;
the sun offers a few final days of light,
before hurrying apples and grapes to one more
ripening and
      then, one day soon,
        the sweetness of heavy wine.

It's time.
Whoever now has no home will build no more,
as things will become other things, like a translation
that forgets, word for pallid word,
      how rivers flow only one way.

Whoever is now alone will remain so,
      and, being alone, will wake each day
      into a dread quiet.

Sometimes the eyes
open in a foreign place, and to read
or write long letters
is a geometry
for sleeplessly wandering streets and alleyways
late into the evening
as leaves rasp across asphalt.

ODE TO PAXIL

Paramour, discrete, I'll mouth your name
when the day's a dazzle of lists and panic

and thus violence takes so many events unto itself—
the sound of a refrigerator door closing,

a bottle of wine upturned,
its contents flowering into the sink.

The pen is the right hand
clicking and clicking and clicking.

Morning's failures are no longer unique
as the books on the shelves haw and

crack like a radio on a sailboat far off
the coast of Halifax. Show me the way to go home.

Remember when we wanted the best
for everyone? And then. And then.

There are so many of us now, too many
for everyone to be recollected—I should say

saved—so time doesn't stand
at attention, or heap into a pile.

It overwhelms us, as humidity overwhelms
the chickens in the pasture, which collapse

one by feathered one—each their eyes, their whitening
tongues, covered with dust. The young girl's forearm

blossoms with burns and scars. She would
say the body's no song. Do tell.

A gaunt, carved monolith in Northern Iraq
unsepulchered, its great jaws unclamped,

awaits some once-intended moment
its secrets shaped in stone by a forgotten hand.

Standing on a distant hill, its weather is all its own.
Archeologists snap their photographs and later

they'll eat cucumber sandwiches and visualize
coins placed upon the eyelids, right then left.

WHY I LEFT VIENNA

Say it straight:

When memory
is a kind of house— the body bends and

the shape of the shoulder blade spells irretrievable.

What distances are
mine, at last, when I inherit a shaded
life, but a poor
way of speaking?

The key in the door turns clockwise.
Water ripples in a pitcher on the table.

And who will say they knew of me
in the tangled gestures of July's
necessary light?

My friend opens a bottle that smells
of elderberries and indecision, then
rests his glass on *Pierre Bonnard: The Late Interiors.*

And what has ever been as suddenly naked
as a painter's wife stepping from the bath?
There's a word for this.
The light through the window hurts my eyes.

LAZARUS CHORALE

The people in the street clamor for levitation.

To be sent for is not the same
      as invitation.
Who will speak for whom? Let them be, the dead.
Or, consider, what loneliness isn't enough
      to keep a stone in place.

To come forth is to come back and know the cold,
      cold water rushing over
empty cans in the alleyway.

The body is no bed, and the fingernails continue to grow.
Beneath the noonday sun, the lips are still blue
      and hunger hollows the eyes.

A mother drags her children inside. Shadows
      tattoo the cracked pavement.

Let the curtain rise on the third day.
That theater, today, solitary
and cruel as
      any specific space,
the chairs all velvety plush.

We'll make our getaway clean, desperate.

Fade me to black.
The next trick's all yours.

ROMANTIC MACHINE

Tenderness has its own rhetoric. When
I grasp your hand, it means, *how could
revisions ever end?*

Placing my fist
across your eyebrow means, *here is the horizon
memory takes.* My palms against
my chest means, *the world's a gossip,
and we are such tiny thirsts.*
Go on.

REFRAIN

The week is an almanac of denials—
    sow, not reap;
        rain, not sun.

    The fetid water from a French restaurant's kitchen
      flows into the gutter's grates.

      And as in any small town
nothing lonelies like the self.
      Calling it uncanny doesn't
      help or so

Narcissus tells himself
the same story over and over and I wonder what
      boredom is to him.
Is it a strange man's
      kisses in quick succession that leaves
a wine-red lesion on the hand? Why not
                lift the eyes?

I was thinking of repetition.
The body at middle age is an echo
trapped underground in some
      forgotten subway tunnel—
    the old "what of" that is
some seismographic recording too late,
too late. The sign says
you are open and, for a moment, means it.

Hold, hold, mutters the ghost on the stair.
　　　For night to be anything but
the uneven first blush of a bluish hour
dismantled in late talk, the cold air disembodies.

Below my window, a woman grasps her love like a new
　　　　screenplay. Dawn, when it comes, is still
　　　　the very shape
　　　　　　of surprise; it starts like a guilty thing.

　　　A man in a blue serge suit—I didn't know
they still made them—coughs into his sleeve. The torn
and faded poster for Fritz Lang's *Scarlet*
　　　　　　Street frames
　　　　just how much past has passed.

Some days are like that: heavy painted canvases
laid alongside the walls of lofts
　　　　in the meatpacking district.

　　　　　　Once I was afraid, not of dying
but of the fat-bellied blue jays
that scream and dive and scream and dive.
My friend is right not to mention phobias
and fixations and the times
　　　　she spent tied to a hospital bed.

As I watch, several tan men scrub with wire brushes
the bronze bricks of the Park Avenue armory among
　　　　the shadows of an unfortunate September.

LANGUAGE POEM

It is raining. Outside the window, that is to say, beyond the glass. Where else? There is a tree outside the window. It is raining into the tree. This is not something we say. But it is true.

I think to ask, *what is the first word you remember remembering?* Perhaps I'll text you.

The door closes behind my wife as she leaves to do some shopping. I hear a voice, or think I do, say these lines as I read them over, and my throat muscles move. I cannot feel them, but I know it to be the case. Or so I have read. I do not feel them, these muscles, as muscles, unless I have been screaming, which I do not do often. Enough. I worry: *it doesn't count.* What is a real voice? Start there. That is my real voice, the woman said. To the letter.

To be grammatical is to be the same, or, I want to say, similar—as when it is raining outside and the television screen reflects the wall, the window, the water rushing from plugged gutters and draining against the sill. Then the television comes on—I pushed a button—and it is raining, perhaps across the plains in a John Ford film. Inside, outside.

I write a word into my palm, then close my fist. The house is empty and calm. No one comes when I call.

TURBO NOIR

In a city of steep hills and jagged compromise,
            winning tastes of broken glass.

So, to deny nothing more of the unknowable
than an astonishing speed—
                I hold my left hand
           before my face.

The everyday chronicles the abandoned.
           Tell a secret, drop a dime, sing,
Pigeon, or squeal. Whichever.

We wake to each new scattering. Told
           between the lines
ways of spelling *without*
shape the story
           between us.

Above the wrist,

there are fine white hairs—
 and a woman
           in a wide-brimmed hat strikes a match
           beneath a flickering streetlight.
The picture frame blurs at the edge. She walks off.
More than economics, vanishing's a slow talent,
           that's why the city has a wharf.

There are three knocks on the door
to an empty office in which a lost address
with no body is written down on a legal pad.

And in the longing that everyone has a place,
a neon sign outside some dive bar
snaps into focus, and belief mouths
a thinly veiled threat.

III.

THE PSYCHIC LIVES OF ANIMALS

Now it is raining.
     There's a clarity that makes so long
a life. Again, then, the outside-it-all
and a guarantee
               of some exquisite
curse to hate the days you live,
     hate them as you live them,
that is, the manner of how you spend
     the hours. In the deep grass,

     the quiet animals: their eyes slow
     and narrow beneath yellow lids.
     There, one finds no home.

My back sways beneath
     a weight of memory, what

comes with the dream of the lost brother
and the disappointed light of late February.

The fragile bones of birds' wings
     foretell a sleepy anger
in their own good time.

               By now,
there's nothing to summon back.
The arrow is pointed skyward.
Every angle is terrifying.

ANGER ANALOGUE

When you dreamed the dream of the tree ablaze
        the blackbirds ignited, one by one, their wings
iridescent in a sickening light.

And the truth is, truth speaks in so many
        sullen ways. Blind rage begets
a blank trouble.

In the song, the birds are still falling—
        there is nothing there to stop them.
Smoke, they say, gets in your eyes.

And, despite all understanding, you want the wanting,
comfortable as a name, familiar
as a white scar across the knuckle.
I place my hand upon your wrist
and place your wrist upon the table.

And so he painted the inside of the sky. He first painted
it gray and cave-shaped—and everywhere he looked the
world passed over itself: stars or wind or rain or sound or
smoke. Sometimes reverie is an accusation. In the cracks
at the edges where the paint yellowed and flaked, an ash
tree bloomed, and for a moment the leaves decided not to
speak out, but to point towards a place no one could quite
see. Then he laid down in the long, wet grass and slept for
weeks and weeks and never once thought about raising
the dead, or spilling wine from open scars, or believing
whatever wasn't some slightly sad dream in which everyone
he knows and everyone he doesn't know watches the same
silent movie in which a woman wearing a gingham dress
slowly lifts a young boy into the back of a model-T Ford
over and over again.

A BRIEF HISTORY OF THE UNIVERSE

nothing

more than

this

SCREEN TIME

And do not let the film end just yet,
     the final frame against the pearlescent screen:
     winter crosses left to right,
the credits between me and there, snow catching
     upon a Russian soldier's epaulet. Do not strike
the scene now. Linger like the figure in the painting
who never
utters a sound from his half-opened
mouth, or like a curse
remembered from childhood.

Let the unkind light of the stage lamps stay lit,
     and someone else's vision
     guide us along
the edges of whatever's leftover.

What did you expect? To live through
anything other
than one more ending, a perpetual loop
that recollects each splice,
     and the handsome stranger who enters
       the hallway again
       and again, each time the first time.

Stretch me thinner and thinner to become a quiet,
     a shuttered place, become
a ghost to my own papered chamber.

ORANGES ON THE TABLE,
WATER IN THE KETTLE

Still, it's a surprise to find oneself each day
waking up in a room with windows,
with a door, or two, because it could be
otherwise. Strange that it is not strange when
it could be we wake, each of us, singly, arrived
with eyes opened, at some other place, another moment.
But, honestly, all moments are another.
Even now and then, again, now.

For how long am I a certain shape of space:
the sun above it all, beyond slate roofs
and rusted gutters, past those few clouds,
and night on its way?
I look east.

PENTECOST

Afternoon is a Ouija board pointing yes or no. Then,
on their own, letters
        form some address,
a friend's, perhaps, one flown somewhere
        across the sea. A phone rings and rings and rings.

The air fills with pollen and the new leaves
        of Linden trees.

And when the lake is a vague blue
            and the sailboats almost inconsolably
        happy, when the sunlight's
        so relentlessly itself, nothing either moves or
            vanishes,
when the small voice of a mourning dove
        empties into the landscape falling through
space for hours and hours, who's to say

there will be no going back or second thoughts?

HE WILL CLOSE HIS EYES AND
THINK OF SPAIN

A man sits at the window watching two jays drift from wire
to wire while a dead woman's song filters from an upstairs
apartment. *I'm crazy, crazy for feeling so blue…*
    There will be the sound of hammers in just a moment.
He will sleep and wake and sleep and wake.

●

Contradictions shape a given day: I want to remember
what it is like to be tired of beauty, to taste the slow going
of vivid facts, the clumsiness of mouthing a location in an
unfamiliar language. Lips meeting and parting the way

a twinge in the leg breaks up forgettable dreams into sheets
of ice floating off towards the horizon. Where it can, a
sense of not-quite regret filters through events like sunlight
or like change. Undeniably, limitations form every sound of
every syllable. This, we are given to say, is the body.

In a small back alley studio, in the middle of the last
century, a painter pulls back the blanket covering the
half-finished scene of a table filled with daylilies and water
glasses. A brush glides forward, catching for a moment on
the canvas weave, then is flicked back to the pallet. The
hand grows tired, eventually.

●

Consider the broad light of knowing something, anything even so obscure as the exact pollen count produced in seven acres of alfalfa in a field in southern Maine or the weight of a coin produced in the Sung dynasty. Intent fashions a space out of all our uncertainty; it takes dominion everywhere. It makes a sound: a sharp intake of breath, a tiny door opening.

•

Like small errant fish disappearing in kelp beds, everything scatters. What becomes the flesh? Whatever it is, I want it all, and now. Then, still, enough.

•

And the man at the window had once wanted to become his beliefs, whatever they were, to walk everywhere within them, their comfort, to have them shoot outward in all directions. But he faltered and forgot their possibilities, if he ever knew them, or there was static on the line (the jays, again) and he had misheard. Some wishes tell themselves and the sun still shines all day. His eyes close.

IV.

SON ET LUMIÈRE

"I wander all night in my vision…"
                    —Walt Whitman

All night I walk as a ghost
among the lost and the living.
From the river, swollen past its banks,
up through to the city's center,

there where people ebb and flow, singly,
or in groups, choosing their means
haltingly, like a nearly forgotten catechism,
call it love or anger, I make my way.

There are nights woven from thick hours
spun during daylight's fretfulness.
Stand out of the sun, someone says
and evening ripens like a fig.

Think now of what fashions the hour:
what comes from what. The moon
waxes and wanes. I didn't ask
to be here, to become a form
that becomes its own end.

What if life is just that: leaning at the horizon?
By that I mean a wished-for hurtling forward,
the only solution a dissolution.

The streetlights each curve downward
and stretch far past the bridges and avenues,

past the café where the student opens then
closes her book. *More light*, she says to the waiter.
Some days it's easier to tally
those furtive thoughts that have no future
rather than those, like the noon sun's glare,

that swallow every shadow beneath our feet.
I place a branch upon the palm of my right hand
and cannot in certain terms prove to myself
I am not dreaming. The smell of burnt pork
carries through the alleyway behind an atelier.

A man I want to believe walked past a bay window.
I wanted to believe most of all that he remained
there because it proves, simply, I am at this place
at any ordinary hour of any ordinary day.
This is what it means to be someone.

If I were to speak just now,
my throat would catch, my voice
falter and stammer. *It couldn't be
colder*, a father on some sitcom
playing in the 24-hr health club insists.

On the contrary, there's no end
to how we never do measure
the shape of enough, my friend.

Divide what you will listen to
by the ratio of all you have lost.

From mud and sticks and twine and error,
I built a shameful twin
to move through a squalid winter,
to share all manner of guilt.

I'll watch as he steps forth,
smelling of ash and amnesia, of sex
and leaves, of all I needn't feel.
This one will never sleep nor walk a crooked mile.

I forget it isn't simply a way to avoid
another's outrage. Sitting quietly, hands
folded, one over the other: it only seemed
like waiting. The fingernails lengthening
and hardening into fine gray slate.

Nextness fills window after window
—one scene, then another—
with a disappointment or wonder.
An eyelid flutters involuntarily.
Not even this in vain.

With our eyes we distinguish
everything—sleep from day, thus
days from weeks to years. And if time,
then loss—hence love. There are gifts
we are given so they may be taken away.

At the edge of the forest beside the city
wild boars, black as pitch,
drag small animals into the brush.
Why is this night different from all other nights?

Alright, a still life, perhaps:
Compotier Flush with Cruelty.
Paint, a pear, glass, and so much green
       aghast with longing.
It makes a claim, already, for beauty—
a reason for looking that telescopes
these angles past the edges of the table.

It needn't have been so bad, and it isn't, not really.
Given enough time. This afternoon, for example,
there were lemons in a bowl
filled with water and the scent
hung thickly on thick red curtains. I slept. And so.

Cigarette smoke brushing the skin is enough.
The one maple tree in the yard is enough.
The crow on the dock at the lake's edge
       and the rowboat, moving and rocking,
and the long cloud above, these are enough.
Your breath, even now, is enough.

In late summer, from a dry field will come
some persistent tune, locusts, perhaps,
or the husk of longing tends toward a dwelling-place,

some subtler music to frame the way
onward. All of it anyway to read the boundaries

beyond which nothing is found. So, tonight
on the subway, a businessman slips into sleep,
his left eye half open. Who would place a kiss there?
His breathing the very human sound of limitation
and what, being human, it allows us.

I glance along the roof of the train. A bulb flickers
above a young woman in combat boots. The dog
at her feet is not well, pants and trembles.
I imagine calling out name after name until she
turns her head.
In this light everything looks bad, but some things worse.

I blink once, twice as I step out of the florescence
of the underground station and move through
a crowd of teenagers, workers. Every word,
for a moment, is other, unrecognized. I am now
another space passing through the present.

Almost over now, says a bartender,
reaching for a beer soaked rag.
A dime descends elegantly through a lawyer's rum
and coke to the bottom of the glass.

It's easy to become lost among all these objects,
among dishes and chairs, among pens and porcelain,

books, and dried flowers—the sickening smell of incense
and Mop & Glo hovering about it all. And more.
I can choose to be here and I do. Or I go

to an all-night diner, steel counters and padded booths.
The coffee's sweet and thick with milk and
the mind's anywhere. Everywhere.
Two women, both with gray hair, sit
near the door eating toast and jam while the air

around them trembles in neon. It's a sign. Snow
begins to fall and it would keep falling, were the earth
not there to stop it. Gravity catches us all, beginning
and end. Some day. The material life of objects merit
praise, whatever we can muster. It provides a sheen.
I go outside again to meet it.

Some indifferent late winter, one irreconcilable night,
what steps forward is what, in passing, any can call
a world—not that these are the only options that are,
as they are, but one possible sounding you or I might

organize, as an old man standing on a bridge passes
a hand back and forth before the face of what
we recognize, willingly or otherwise, and arcs
into a dialect or patois. Saying so becomes it.

From what happens and does not happen
we collect ourselves; for instance,

lying abed, eyes rolling, given to sleep
or stupor. How did it get so late so quickly?

In the afternoon, on the subway platform,
a beautiful stranger with a microphone
asked me about my favorite fragrance.
Now the scent of alder and pine, wet pavement
and burnt espresso adjust each small response.

Then I forget the time. Head tipped back
I close my eyes and the dark becomes darker.
Or perhaps there behind the lids it all
starts over. I acted as if.

Streaming from the battered doors of an old club comes
Patsy Cline's voice, high, almost lost. It reaches
the street where a cab sits and waits, the meter running.
The smoke from the exhaust rises, becomes the snow.
To be all these possibilities, I light another cigarette.

Where right now is that twin? I wonder.
Would I become him, now or ever?
That's what the city's for. Some evenings, hope blooms
like rent boys along the middle avenue
in early spring. But people also sleep and dream.

There is this life, thrown or found,
it takes a shape and makes its time. Yet,
why becomes *want* again and again.

In a hotel lobby, someone cleans a mirror
cut into the shape of the downtown skyline.

There's a genre of hours—some hone,
some wreak havoc; others circle and circle, then tire.
Some knit a home from heartbeat and expectation.
I conjure a breath, first, then some sounds.
What remains? Wait for it, now.

People move in and out of doors
without a story, without a promise.
Still, there's the moon and those stars.
Empty branches scratch a private glance
against brick buildings filled with lives
I will never live too much to find.

Three floors up, a figure stands at a kitchen window.
I am almost tired enough and yet it's colder now.
Belonging's not like a song, but a murmur.
And when, as it does, evening comes,
there's a chance the sounds will not let up
and the night's so long.

ENVOI

I will read to you, read to you from
the book of forthcoming, a text
        in variations:
     an index to ask
     of what
you meant to answer, but
then was gone like a breath
     or a hope.
Before there was any of this,
       there was you.

NOTES

Most of the poems of this collection are ekphrastic in nature. At the same time, I often felt a sense of a definite person with whom a poem is in conversation, explicitly or implicitly. The following dedications seek to acknowledge those conversations, encounters, and debts.

"Film Threat" is for Michael Kelleher

"Rashomon Affect" is for Patricia Willis

"Caravaggio Dreams" is for Roberto Tejada

"The Picture of JSB in a Prospect of Lady Boys" is for Joshua Brown

"If Nancy Were a de Kooning" is for Nancy Kuhl

"In a Blue Mood" is for Steve Evans

"Air Guitar" is for Graham Foust

"The Weather Almost" is for Marianne LaFrance and Megan Mangum

"Tourneuresque" is for Elizabeth Willis

"After Rilke" is for William Heyen

"Why I Left Vienna" is for Jean-Jacques Poucel

"Refrain" is for Cathy Eisenhower

"Language Poem" is for Joel Bettridge

"Turbo Noir" is for Caleb Smith and Jennifer Mellon

"A Brief History of the Universe" is for Simon Cutts

"Pentecost" is for Leland de la Durantaye

AUTHOR

Richard Deming's first collection of poems, *Let's Not Call It Consequence*, won the Norma Farber Award from the Poetry Society of America and was a finalist for the Connecticut Book Award. He is also the author of *Listening on All Sides: Towards an Emersonian Ethics of Reading*. In 2012, he was awarded the Berlin Prize by the American Academy in Berlin. He is currently Director of Creative Writing at Yale University.